ARKANSAS

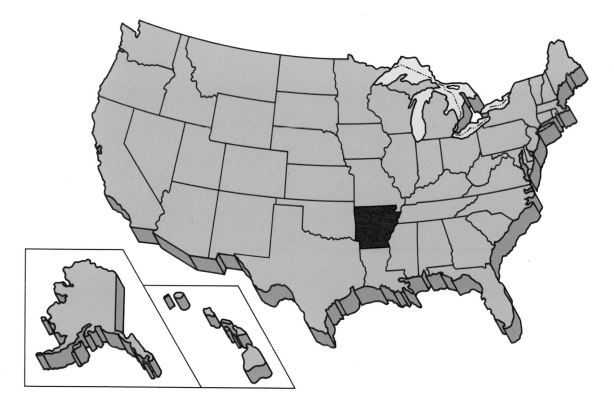

ARKANSAS

Domenica Di Piazza

Lerner Publications Company

Cover photograph by Buddy Mays / Travel Stock.

The glossary that begins on page 68 gives definitions of words shown in **bold type** in the text.

LIBRARY OF CONGRESS
CATALOGING-IN-PUBLICATION DATA
Di Piazza, Domenica.
    Arkansas / Domenica Di Piazza.
        p.   cm. — (Hello U.S.A.)
    Includes index.
    ISBN 0-8225-2742-1 (lib. bdg.)
    1. Arkansas—Juvenile literature. [1. Arkansas.]
    I. Title. II. Series.
    F411.3.D5   1994
    976.7—dc20   93-33391
                                         CIP
                                          AC

Manufactured in the United States of America

1 2 3 4 5 6 – I/JR – 99 98 97 96 95 94

This book is printed on acid-free, recyclable paper.

CONTENTS

A family digs for diamonds at Crater of Diamonds State Park.

Did You Know . . . ?

❑ Crater of Diamonds State Park in Murfreesboro, Arkansas, is the only place in North America where visitors can dig for diamonds and keep what they find.

❑ The city of Texarkana belongs to Arkansas—and to Texas. Many people have their picture taken in front of the city's post office, which straddles the state line.

❑ Farmers in Hope, Arkansas, grow the world's biggest watermelons. Some have weighed as much as 260 pounds (118 kilograms).

❑ Hot Springs National Park in western Arkansas was once a sacred bathing site for Native Americans. They called the region Valley of the Vapors because of the steam that rises off the area's pools of naturally hot springwater.

❑ Little Rock, Arkansas's capital, was named for a small rock formation on the south side of the Arkansas River. French explorer Bernard de la Harpe chose the name in 1722 to set the settlement apart from a nearby village identified by a larger rocky ridge.

A Trip Around the State

AHR-kuhn-saw or ahr-KAN-suhs? For many years, people disagreed about how to pronounce the name of this southern state. More than 100 years ago, Arkansas's state government decided that the official pronunciation would be AHR-kuhn-saw. With its many hot springs, sparkling lakes, and forested mountain peaks, Arkansas is a beautiful state—no matter how you say it.

Arkansas has six neighbors. To the north is Missouri. On the east, the Mississippi River separates Arkansas from the states of Tennessee and Mississippi. Louisiana borders Arkansas on the south, and Texas and Oklahoma lie to the west.

Rocks form a natural archway in the mountains of western Arkansas.

The western part of Arkansas is rugged and mountainous, while the eastern and southern parts of the state are mostly flat. Northwestern land regions include the Ozark Plateau, the Arkansas Valley, and the Ouachita Mountains. The fertile soil of the Mississippi Plain covers most of eastern Arkansas. The lowlands of the Coastal Plain spread across the southwestern corner of the state.

Forests cover much of the Ozark Plateau, also known as the Ozarks. This region is part of a vast **plateau** (high flatland) that stretches across several states. Fast-running rivers have carved deep, narrow passageways called gorges between the region's limestone ridges. Farmers tend fruit orchards and raise livestock such as cattle and poultry in the Ozarks.

MISSOURI

•Fayetteville

Buffalo River

White River

Saint Francis River

OZARK PLATEAU

Jonesboro

TENNESSEE

•Fort Smith

ARKANSAS VALLEY

▲ MAGAZINE MOUNTAIN

OUACHITA MOUNTAINS

N. Little Rock

LITTLE ROCK ★

MISSISSIPPI PLAIN

OKLAHOMA

HOT SPRINGS NATIONAL PARK

Pine Bluff•

Arkansas River

Mississippi River

MISSISSIPPI

COASTAL PLAIN

Red River

ARKANSAS

—— Regional boundary

Miles
0   30   60

0   30   60
Kilometers

TEXAS

LOUISIANA

N

The Arkansas Valley is named for the Arkansas River, which winds its way southeastward to the Mississippi River. The valley is rich in underground deposits of coal and natural gas. The region also boasts the state's highest point—Magazine Mountain, which reaches 2,753 feet (839 meters).

The Ouachita Mountains are well known for their underground springwaters. People from all over the United States come to Hot Springs National Park. Here, warm water bubbles to the surface and is piped to bathhouses, where people relax in pools of the steamy water. Visitors to the region also enjoy lakes, rivers, and forested sandstone peaks.

Fishers take part in a contest in Little Rock. The city lies along the Arkansas River.

Rice is a major crop in the Mississippi Plain.

Along the banks of the Mississippi River in eastern Arkansas spreads the flat land of the Mississippi Plain. Years of flooding from the Mississippi River have made the region's soil very fertile. As the floodwaters withdrew, they left behind **sediment,** or layers of sand and dirt. Land enriched by river flooding is known as a **delta,** and many Arkansans call the Mississippi Plain the Delta. Farmers in the Delta plant soybeans, rice, cotton, and wheat.

13

Many people earn a living from agriculture on the Coastal Plain as well. Most farmers in this region raise livestock, but some plant tomatoes, watermelons, and other fruits. Swamps and bayous, or slow-moving streams, break up the Coastal Plain's vast pine forests, which are a major source of timber. The state's largest oil wells are also found in the region.

Arkansas's chief waterways include the Mississippi, Arkansas, White, Red, and Saint Francis rivers. Dams, which block and control the flow of water, have been

A waterfall tumbles down a rocky ledge.

built across many of Arkansas's rivers. The dams help prevent flooding by holding back water in large storage areas called reservoirs. In fact, most of Arkansas's biggest lakes are reservoirs.

The weather in Arkansas is generally warm. Summer temperatures in the south and east average about 84° F (29° C), while the mountains are usually several degrees cooler. The same is true in winter, when the average January temperature is around 45° F (7° C) in the lowlands and only 39° F (4° C) in the highlands of the northwest.

Every year the state receives about 49 inches (124 centimeters) of **precipitation** (rain, sleet, and snow). Only about 6 inches (15 cm) of snow fall each year, mostly in the Ozarks and in the Ouachita Mountains.

Yellow jasmines *(above)* and magnolias *(top right)* thrive in Arkansas's warm climate.

Precipitation helps many kinds of plants grow in Arkansas. About half the land is wooded. Loblolly and shortleaf pine trees thrive in southern Arkansas. In the northwestern mountains, hardwood trees such as oaks and hickories grow alongside shortleaf pines. Cypress trees sprawl in the state's bayous and swamps.

Flowering trees in the state include magnolias, redbuds, and dogwoods. Bellflowers, yellow jasmines, and other wildflowers bloom throughout the state.

Arkansas's varied landscape provides homes for many wild animals. Alligators live in the state's swamps. Deer, bears, bobcats, and foxes find shelter in forests.

Night creatures called armadillos dig their underground homes in warm parts of the state. Rabbits, squirrels, opossums, muskrats, raccoons, skunks, and weasels make homes throughout Arkansas. With so much natural beauty, Arkansas lives up to its nickname—the Natural State.

Armadillo

Alligator

Early Indians built giant earthen mounds in Arkansas. Some of the mounds served as burial sites. Others were the foundations of temples and homes.

Arkansas's Story

The first people to come to what is now Arkansas arrived in the area at least 12,000 years ago. They were hunters who moved from place to place looking for wild game. The ancestors of American Indians, these early peoples found the region richly forested. Buffalo, deer, and bears roamed freely. Mammoths—huge elephants with giant tusks—were also plentiful.

Several thousand years later, people called bluff dwellers were making permanent homes in caves and under rock overhangs in the Ozarks. They hunted deer and wild turkeys, using darts thrown from a grooved stick. They also fished the rivers and planted corn, squash, pumpkins, and sunflowers in the rich soil along creeks.

Other Indians had settled near the Mississippi River by about 1000 B.C. They lived in villages and planted corn, pumpkins, and tobacco. Called mound builders, these Indians built giant earthen hills for religious ceremonies. Powerful leaders lived on top of mounds built just for them.

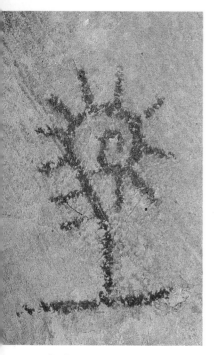

At Petit Jean State Park in northwestern Arkansas, visitors can see images painted on cave walls by Indians thousands of years ago.

By A.D. 1500, the bluff dwellers and mound builders had disappeared. No one is quite sure why, but experts think that disease, warfare, or lack of rain may have killed many people and forced others to flee their homes.

At about the same time, in 1541, a Spanish expedition led by Hernando de Soto reached the eastern shore of the Mississippi River. The group spent nearly a month building canoes to carry the explorers, their horses, and their main food supply—a herd of pigs—across the river. For almost a year, the explorers traveled through what is now Arkansas, hoping to find gold. But they didn't find any riches, and by the time the group left the area, all the pigs had run off into the woods.

A captured Indian guide leads Spanish explorer Hernando de Soto and his men to a place where they can safely cross the Mississippi River.

The Quapaw, like other Indians in Arkansas, made arrows and other weapons from wood or bone.

Groups of American Indians, some of them descended from the mound builders, were living in what is now Arkansas at the time de Soto explored the area. Members of the Caddo nations (or tribes) made tall, cone-shaped homes in villages in the southwest. For food they grew crops and hunted buffalo. To travel by river, they carved huge logs into dugout canoes.

The Quapaw and the Osage nations eventually entered what is now Arkansas from the Ohio River valley far to the east. The Osage hunted throughout much of what is now northern Arkansas. The Quapaw built rectangular, bark-covered homes in villages near the

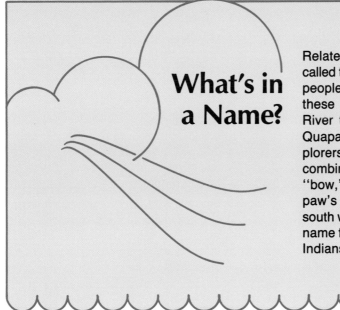

What's in a Name?

Related to the Osage Indians, the Quapaw called themselves *Ugakhpa,* or "downstream people." The name refers to the fact that these Indians lived along the Mississippi River to the south of the Osage. But the Quapaw were known by early French explorers as the Arkansas. This name is a combination of *arc,* a French word meaning "bow," and *ansa,* a word from the Quapaw's language meaning "people of the south wind." The state of Arkansas takes its name from the French label for the Quapaw Indians.

Mississippi River. They raised crops and crafted fine pottery.

After de Soto's journey across what is now Arkansas, more than 100 years passed before another European set foot in the area. Looking to expand France's fur-trading empire in North America, French explorers began traveling down the Mississippi River.

In 1682 French explorer René-Robert Cavelier de La Salle claimed the entire Mississippi River valley for France. He named the region Louisiana, after Louis XIV, the king of France. Four years later, Henri de Tonti, who had traveled with La Salle's party, returned to the Arkansas River and built Arkansas Post. This fur-trading site was the first permanent white settlement in Arkansas.

The French traders depended on Indians to supply furs. The Caddo, for example, traded their crops

Arkansas Post was visited mostly by French fur traders until the early 1700s, when settlers first arrived in the area.

with other Indian nations in exchange for animal furs. The Caddo then gave the furs to French traders, receiving manufactured goods such as cloth, beads, and guns in return. When the French sold the furs in Europe, they made huge profits.

Few Europeans settled in Arkansas in the 1700s. Near Arkansas Post, the Arkansas River often flooded, destroying crops. So the settlers had to depend mostly on hunting and fishing for food. Every year they sent bear's oil, salted buffalo meat, and animal hides south to the growing town of New Orleans in exchange for everyday necessities.

By 1770 only 8 families, about 30 soldiers, and a handful of outlaws were living at Arkansas Post. More people came to the area after France sold Louisiana to the United States in 1803 in a deal called the Louisiana Purchase. The purchase added a vast stretch of land, including what is now Arkansas, to the United States.

Settlers from crowded states in the eastern United States flocked west to buy land, which was sold at low prices by the U.S. government. By 1819 more than 14,000 white people were living in what is now Arkansas. Many settled in northern and western Arkansas, where river flooding was not as big a problem as it was at Arkansas Post. That same year, the U.S. government established the Territory of Arkansas.

As more and more settlers came to Arkansas, the Indians' way of life changed dramatically. Most of the newcomers, for example, were farmers. They chopped down woodlands to make room for crops, and they drove away much of the wild game the Indians depended on for food. The settlers also carried diseases to which Indians had never been exposed, so many Native Americans died.

At first, the U.S. government made **treaties,** or agreements, with the Indians in Arkansas. The treaties set aside **reservations,** or areas of land for the Native Americans to live on. But the government eventually broke many of the treaties, claiming more land for settlers. In some cases, the government bought land from the Indians at low prices.

The Arkansas Traveler

Many of the pioneers who settled in the Ozarks and in the Ouachita Mountains came from the Appalachian Mountains in the eastern United States. To their new Arkansas homes, the mountaineers brought a rich tradition of storytelling. Tales were told to pass the time around the family fireplace or at the gristmill, where farmers waited for their corn to be ground. Full of exaggeration, the stories were often set to music. One famous tale, known as "The Arkansas Traveler," was first told in the 1840s and still survives as a popular song and fiddler's tune.

A traveler was riding by that day
And stopped to hear him practicing away.
The cabin was afloat and his feet were wet.
But still the old man didn't seem to fret.

So the stranger said, "Now the way it seems to me,
You'd better mend your roof," said he.
But the old man said as he played away,
"I couldn't mend it now, it's a rainy day."

The traveler replied, "That's all quite true,
But this, I think, is the thing for you to do.
Get busy on a day that is fair and bright,
Then patch the old roof till it's good and tight."

But the old man kept on a-playin' his reel,
And tapped the ground with his leathery heel.
"Get along," said he, "for you give me a pain;
My cabin never leaks when it doesn't rain."

During the 1830s, the U.S. government wanted more land for white settlers. So the U.S. Army forced the Indians in Arkansas and other southeastern territories and states to move west to a place called Indian Territory in what is now Oklahoma. Many Native Americans, forced to walk the journey, died from disease and lack of food and water. The suffering was so great that the route became known as the Trail of Tears.

By 1835 Arkansas had more than 50,000 white settlers, enough to apply for statehood. On June 15, 1836, Arkansas joined the Union as the 25th state.

Most Arkansans were farmers who worked small plots of land.

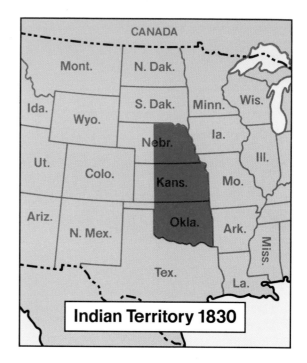

Indian Territory 1830

But in the Mississippi and Arkansas river valleys, farmers had begun to build huge cotton **plantations.** Slaves brought to America from Africa did most of the back-breaking work of clearing the land and planting cotton on these large farms. By 1860 at least one out of four people in Arkansas was a black slave.

In the northern United States, slavery was illegal. The North tried to pressure the South to end slavery. Instead, several Southern states formed a new country, the Confederate States of America (the Confederacy). In the Confederacy, slavery was legal.

Slaves worked long hours picking cotton off thorny stems by hand.

Runaway Negro in Jail.

WAS committed to the Jail of Saline county, as a runaway, on the 8th day of June, 1851, a negro man, who says his name is JOHN, and that he belongs to *Henry Johnson*, of Desha county, Ark. He is aged about 24 or 25 years, straight in stature, quick spoken, looks very fierce out of his eyes, and plays on the fiddle. Had on, when apprehended, white cotton pants, coarse cotton shirt, and black hat. The owner is hereby notified to come forward, prove property, and pay the expenses of committal and advertisement, otherwise the said negro will be dealt with according to law.   THOMAS PACK, *Sheriff and Jailor of Saline county.*

Benton, June 21, 1851.   7—26w.

Pay up! Pay up!!

ALL persons indebted to the undersigned whose notes and accounts are *now due*, are requested to call and *pay up*, by the 1st day of July next.   JOHN D. ADAMS.

June 13, 1851.   5—

Slaves were considered property and did not have the right to come and go as they pleased. They could be thrown in jail for running away from their owners.

White Arkansans were split. Compared to some of its Southern neighbors, Arkansas had few slaves. Most of these slaves worked plantations in the southern and eastern parts of the state, where many people wanted Arkansas to join the Confederacy. But farmers in northwestern Arkansas didn't depend on slave labor to make a profit and wanted the state to stay in the Union.

Arkansans were forced to choose sides after the Civil War broke out between the North and the South in April 1861. Most of Arkansas's soldiers, about 66,000, fought for the Confederacy. Nearly 15,000 men from northwestern Arkansas, both white and black soldiers, fought for the Union.

Split in Two

Arkansas joined the Confederate States of America in 1861, so most Arkansans sided with the Confederacy during the Civil War. But many people in the northwestern part of the state fought for the Union. The state was officially divided after Union troops captured Little Rock—the state capital—in September 1863. With the Union in control of the state's capital city, Arkansas's Confederate government moved its headquarters to Washington, Arkansas, in the southwestern part of the state. For the rest of the war, Arkansas had two capitals and two governors, one representing the Union and the other the Confederacy.

Union troops guard ammunition and weapons stored at Little Rock.

During the Civil War, many Arkansans lost their homes and jobs. In 1865, after four years of battle, the Confederacy admitted defeat. Southerners began to rebuild their homes and farms during a difficult postwar period called **Reconstruction.**

During this time, U.S. troops from the North moved into Arkansas to oversee the rebuilding of the state. To rejoin the Union, Arkansas had to make slavery illegal and had to allow black men to vote. In 1868 the state was readmitted.

By the late 1800s, after Reconstruction, Arkansas's government had passed a series of new laws making it almost impossible for African American men to vote. Black people also were barred from eating at the same restaurants as white people and from going to the same schools, theaters, and hotels.

GUILTY!

ne of Arkansas's most famous citizens was Isaac Charles Parker, a judge at Fort Smith, Arkansas, from 1875 until 1896. Lying on Arkansas's westernmost boundary, Fort Smith bordered what remained of Indian Territory. Laws in the territory applied only to Native Americans. Bank robbers, bandits, and murderers hoped to make it to the territory to escape the law. On their way, the criminals passed through Fort Smith, giving the town a reputation as a rough place with little law and order.

But Judge Parker, who had control over western Arkansas and Indian Territory, quickly put that idea to rest. When he first arrived in Fort Smith, 18 murderers were awaiting court trials. Of those 18, Parker sentenced 8 to death by hanging, and 1 other was shot as he tried to escape. In Parker's 21-year courtroom career, he sentenced more than 160 men to death, of whom about 80 were actually hanged. Outlaws called Parker the Hanging Judge, and Fort Smith gained a new reputation as Hell on the Border.

In the late 1800s, industry in Arkansas progressed rapidly. Timber companies from northern states, where large forests had already been cut down, headed for Arkansas to log the state's pine forests. Arkansans made money mining bauxite (an ore from which aluminum is made) after it was discovered near Little Rock in 1887. Railroad companies built tracks across the state, and trains carried Arkansas's lumber and mineral products to market. Coal mined in western and southern Arkansas fueled the new trains.

To make more money, railroad companies encouraged people from the East Coast and Europe to settle along Arkansas's new railways. The companies knew that people living near train stations would buy tickets to travel on the railroads and would pay to ship goods to market. Newcomers arrived from eastern states, and **immigrants** came from France, Italy, and Greece. By 1900 Arkansas's population had grown to more than one million people.

Trains *(inset)* **hauled logs to mills** *(above),* **where the wood was sawed into lumber.**

Arkansas's economy continued to grow in the early 1900s. Natural gas was discovered near Fort Smith in 1901. Twenty years later, oil was drilled for the first time in Arkansas, near El Dorado. More forests were cleared in the Delta, and farmers planted fields of cotton, rice, and soybeans across the newly opened land.

Bad weather and a drop in cotton prices meant hard times for

Centered on Arkansas's state flag is a large white diamond. It represents a mine in Murfreesboro, Arkansas—the only diamond mine known to exist in the United States. The 25 white stars show that Arkansas was the 25th state to join the Union.

Residents of Little Rock took to their boats when the Arkansas River flooded the city in the spring of 1927.

many farmers in Arkansas during the 1920s. Floods in 1927 drowned livestock and destroyed millions of acres of cropland in the Arkansas and Mississippi river valleys. Just three years later, a terrible drought hit Arkansas. Without enough water, crops withered and died.

The Great Depression of the 1930s affected people across the nation. Banks failed, businesses closed, and workers lost their jobs. Prices for cotton dropped so low that many farmers in Arkansas's Delta region couldn't afford to buy enough food to feed their families.

Arkansas's economy began to recover after the United States entered World War II in 1941. Weapons factories opened in Pine Bluff and Jacksonville. Bauxite mining increased in the state because aluminum was needed to make airplanes for the war. And the U.S. military bought Arkansas's oil to fuel airplanes and tanks.

After the war ended in 1945, African Americans across the nation continued to work toward equality. Little Rock became a battleground in this struggle for equal rights, which was known as the **civil rights movement.**

In 1954 the U.S. Supreme Court ruled that it was illegal to prevent black students from attending the same public schools as white students. Three years later, nine African Americans registered for class at Little Rock's all-white Central High School.

Arkansas's governor, Orval Faubus, was against blacks and whites going to school together. President Dwight D. Eisenhower sent U.S. Army troops to Little Rock to make sure the black students were allowed to attend classes. Over time, other public facilities in Arkansas opened their doors to both blacks and whites.

By the 1960s, for the first time in the state's history, more Arkansans were earning money from manufacturing jobs than from farming. New industries came to the state, hiring workers to make everything from bicycles to doors.

In the fall of 1957, U.S. government troops guarded African American students at Central High School in Little Rock.

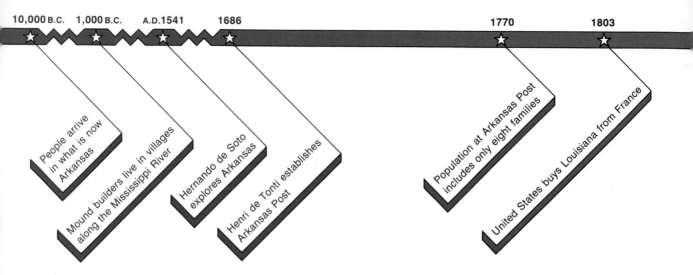

| 10,000 B.C. | 1,000 B.C. | A.D. 1541 | 1686 | 1770 | 1803 |

People arrive in what is now Arkansas

Mound builders live in villages along the Mississippi River

Hernando de Soto explores Arkansas

Henri de Tonti establishes Arkansas Post

Population at Arkansas Post includes only eight families

United States buys Louisiana from France

To help manufacturers get their products to market, Arkansas began a new transportation project. Workers deepened parts of the Arkansas River and built **locks** and dams, so big oceangoing ships could travel the river. The McClellan-Kerr Arkansas River Navigation System was completed in 1971.

Arkansans continue to improve the quality of life in their state. In the 1980s, the state bought more computers for classrooms and expanded science programs at the University of Arkansas. These efforts and others help ensure that Arkansans will have the skills they need for the jobs of the future.

Living and Working in Arkansas

A British traveler named Charles Daubeny toured Arkansas in 1837 and wrote that the only unfriendly treatment he met while in the state was from the dogs. At that time, about 50,000 people lived in Arkansas. The state's population has since grown to 2.3 million. That's 47 times as many Arkansans as when Daubeny visited the state!

Nowadays, four out of five Arkansans (nearly 83 percent) are white people with European ancestors. Almost 16 percent of the state's residents are African American. Together, Asian Americans, Native Americans, and Latinos make up less than 2 percent of the state's population.

More than half of Arkansas's residents live in urban areas, or cities and towns. The state's largest cities are its capital—Little Rock—followed by Fort Smith,

Arkansas's state capitol building is in Little Rock.

Sheriffs are among Arkansas's many service workers.

North Little Rock, Pine Bluff, Jonesboro, and Fayetteville.

Many Arkansans have jobs in these cities. About two out of every three working Arkansans have service jobs, helping people or businesses. Some service workers in Arkansas teach, sell cars and homes, or drive buses and delivery trucks. Others work for the U.S. government at Little Rock Air Force Base, one of the largest military bases in the state.

Service workers in Arkansas also ring up sales at Wal-Mart, one of the nation's largest discount stores, or stock the shelves at Dillard's—a department store known throughout the South. Both of these successful businesses have their headquarters in Arkansas.

A factory worker makes metal parts used for connecting pipes.

Some of the products on store shelves are made in Arkansas. In fact, one out of every four working Arkansans has a manufacturing job. Some workers process foods such as meats, rice, soft drinks, milk, canned vegetables, and feed for farm animals. Others package chicken at Tyson Foods, the nation's largest producer and processor of poultry.

Workers in Arkansas also make air conditioners, electric stoves, refrigerators, lightbulbs, and tele-

visions. Wood and paper products are manufactured from the state's rich supply of timber.

Much of Arkansas's timber is cut down in the Coastal Plain region, where the state's largest oil fields are located. Other major mineral products in Arkansas include natural gas and bromine, which is used in making many kinds of chemicals. Altogether only about 4,000 Arkansans, less than 1 percent of the state's jobholders, earn a living from mining.

Giant rolls of paper *(right)* **are among many wood products made from Arkansas's timber** *(above).*

47

Arkansas ranks among the top 10 states in raising catfish *(above)* and growing cotton *(inset, facing page)*. **Raising chickens and cattle** *(facing page)* **earns the state the most money from agriculture.**

In the 1800s, most people in Arkansas worked on farms. Nowadays only about 1 in 14 people has a job in agriculture. Most raise livestock such as beef and dairy cattle, turkeys, hogs, and broilers (young chickens).

Farmers in Arkansas also plant soybeans, the state's most valuable crop. Other major crops include rice, cotton, hay, corn, and wheat. Grapes, snap beans, tomatoes, and pecans are grown in the state as well.

Arkansas's agricultural bounty makes for good eating. Cooks prepare southern specialties such as deep-fried catfish, fried chicken, cheesy grits, corn bread, and pecan pie. In between meals, there's a lot to see and do in Arkansas.

Outdoor enthusiasts in Arkansas have 45 state parks and 3 national forests to choose from. Tourists explore underground caves at Blanchard Springs Caverns in the Ozark National Forest. Backpackers hike rugged mountain trails in the Ouachita National Forest.

Adventuresome canoeists tackle the rapids on the Buffalo National River in northwestern Arkansas. Along the way, boaters pass spectacular waterfalls, towering bluffs where ancient Indians once lived, and sometimes even an armadillo or two.

History buffs can tour Toltec Mounds State Park near Little Rock to see and learn about ancient Indian mounds. The capital

Canoeists glide along the Buffalo National River.

A visitor explores a cave near Harrison, Arkansas, where underground deposits of minerals form shapes like icicles.

city's Quapaw Quarter features elegant historic homes. Students of the Civil War can visit Pea Ridge National Military Park in northwestern Arkansas, where one of the state's most important battles took place in 1862.

Travelers on the Great River Road, a network of highways following the Mississippi River, pass through the port town of Helena. Here, visitors to the Delta Cultural Center learn about the history of African Americans in the Mississippi River valley. Many people drive south of Helena to tour Arkansas Post National Memorial, the site of the state's earliest European settlement.

An Ozark musician *(above)* **strums his banjo, while young people** *(facing page)* **work on a painting project in Little Rock.**

Across the state in Mountain View, young artists can learn to make applehead dolls or to carve wood at the Ozark Folk Center. At the nearby Ozark Heritage Arts Center in Leslie, audiences listen to Ozark storytellers. In this way, Ozark traditions are preserved and passed on to new generations.

Arkansans of all backgrounds celebrate a rich musical heritage. The state's musicians offer gospel, blues, classical, jazz, and country music. World-famous blues musicians perform at the King Biscuit Blues Festival in Helena each October. Fayetteville hosts the annual Music Festival of Arkansas, welcoming classical and jazz artists each June. And, in April, Mountain View's yearly Fiddle Fest offers lively concerts of toe-tapping country tunes.

Besides enjoying music, Arkansans are also enthusiastic about sports. Basketball fans fill the bleachers to watch the University of Arkansas Razorbacks play basketball. And if you hear someone hollering "Wooooo Pig SOOie!" you're sure to be at a Razorback football game. Many of the team's loyal fans wear red hats in the shape of a razorback hog and cheer for their team with this spirited hog call.

Protecting the Environment

Arkansas raises more broiler chickens than any other state in the country. And the poultry industry in Arkansas is growing as more Americans choose low-fat chicken over beef and pork. But while the industry provides Arkansans with jobs and money, it also pollutes the state's water resources.

Every year Arkansas's broilers produce millions of tons of manure, also known as litter, which poultry farmers must get rid of. The chicken litter contains bacteria, or germs that can cause disease. But the litter also contains chemical nutrients, or food, such as nitrogen and phosphorus. These nutrients help grasses and other plants grow. For this reason, poultry farmers use the litter to fertilize pastures where cattle graze.

Arkansas's poultry farmers raise baby chicks *(facing page, left)* **in chicken coops** *(facing page, top).* **Over time the growing chickens** *(facing page, right)* **produce tons of manure.**

Over the years, so much chicken litter has been spread on the land that it can no longer absorb all the fertilizer. When rain falls, the excess litter is carried into nearby streams, rivers, and lakes. There, the nutrients in the litter cause algae, plants that live just under the water's surface, to grow very thick.

Too much algae reduces the amount of oxygen in a lake or river. Water naturally contains oxygen, which underwater plants and animals need to live. When the algae die, tiny organisms (lifeforms) in the water eat the dead algae and use up a lot of oxygen. The more algae and organisms in the water, the less oxygen fish have to breathe. As a result, fish leave the lake or stream, become sick, or die.

Chicken litter is spread on Arkansas's farmland *(left)*, where rain can carry extra fertilizer into nearby rivers and lakes. Too much fertilizer can choke a waterway with algae *(above)*.

In addition, these waterways feed **aquifers,** or natural underground storehouses of water, from which Arkansans take their drinking water. As the poultry industry has grown, the amount of nitrogen and bacteria has risen in aquifers near poultry farms.

Although people need a small amount of nitrogen in their diet, too much nitrogen can be poisonous. If the amount of nitrogen and disease-carrying bacteria in Arkansas's aquifers continues to increase, this water supply may become unsafe for people to drink.

Water from rivers, streams, and lakes seeps into the ground and helps fill aquifers.

Arkansas's poultry farmers also raise turkeys.

To protect waterways and aquifers, farmers are working with the government and poultry companies in Arkansas to come up with ways to dispose of chicken litter safely. Instead of spreading the litter directly onto the land, poultry farmers are encouraged to collect the litter in covered containers, where it can decay thoroughly. This process, called composting, kills bacteria and reduces the amount of nitrogen in the litter.

The composted litter makes a fertilizer that is less polluting. The fertilizer that Arkansas's poultry farmers don't need for themselves can then be sold to farmers in other parts of the state and across the country.

Young Arkansans help protect a river by cleaning up trash along its banks.

Many Arkansans agree that education is an important part of solving water pollution problems in their state. Besides education programs for farmers, another program teaches young Arkansans about water quality. Using instructions and equipment provided by the Arkansas Water Education Team (WET), students study a waterway in their community over a five-year period.

Through the WET program, students learn how to test water for signs of nutrients, bacteria, and other forms of pollution. If they find that their stream is polluted, students report it to WET, which then tries to discover the source of the pollution. In this way, young people are joining farmers and other Arkansans in the effort to protect Arkansas's water resources for future generations.

Arkansas's Famous People

◀ TESS HARPER

ACTORS

Tess Harper (born 1950), from Mammoth Spring, Arkansas, has appeared in several films, including *Tender Mercies* and *Silkwood*. In 1987 she received an Academy Award nomination for her role in the movie *Crimes of the Heart*.

Alan Ladd (1913–1964) was one of the most popular actors of the 1940s. Born in Hot Springs, Arkansas, he was known for playing soft-spoken tough guys. Ladd's films include *This Gun for Hire* and *Shane*.

Mary Steenburgen (born 1953) grew up in North Little Rock, Arkansas. Steenburgen has appeared in many motion pictures, including *Back to the Future III, Parenthood,* and *Melvin and Howard,* for which she won an Academy Award in 1980.

▲ ALAN LADD

MARY STEENBURGEN ▶

DIZZY DEAN ▶

ATHLETES

Jay Hanna ("Dizzy") Dean (1911–1974), from Lucas, Arkansas, was one of the greatest pitchers in baseball history. During his career, Dean played for the Saint Louis Cardinals and the Chicago Cubs. In 1934 he won 30 games—a record that wasn't broken for 34 years. Dean was elected to the National Baseball Hall of Fame in 1953.

Sidney Moncrief (born 1957) was a guard for the Milwaukee Bucks basketball team in the 1980s. He was twice named the National Basketball Association (NBA) Defensive Player of the Year and was an NBA All-Star player five times during his career. Moncrief is from Little Rock.

Brooks Robinson (born 1937) played third base for the Baltimore Orioles from 1955 to 1977. He won the Gold Glove award 16 times and was named the American League's Most Valuable Player in 1964. The Little Rock native was elected to the National Baseball Hall of Fame in 1983.

◄ SIDNEY MONCRIEF

BROOKS
▼ ROBINSON

◄ JOHN H.
JOHNSON

SAM ▶
WALTON

BUSINESS LEADERS

Helen Gurley Brown (born 1922) is an author from Green Forest, Arkansas. In 1965 she became the editor in chief of *Cosmopolitan* magazine. Under Brown's leadership, the magazine has increased in popularity and sales.

John H. Johnson (born 1918) founded Johnson Publishing Company in the 1940s. Now the largest black-owned firm in the country, the company produces books and magazines, including *Ebony* and *Jet*. Johnson was born in Arkansas City.

Sam Walton (1918–1992) was once called the richest man in America. In 1950 he moved to Bentonville, Arkansas, where he later founded a chain of discount stores called Wal-Mart. The giant retail company now has more than 2,300 locations in the United States and over $55 billion in yearly sales.

MUSICIANS

Johnny Cash (born 1932) is a country-music legend from Kingsland, Arkansas. A singer, songwriter, and guitarist, Cash is best known for his recordings *I Walk the Line* and *At Folsom Prison*. In 1980 Cash was named to the Country Music Hall of Fame.

Al Green (born 1946) began performing gospel songs with his brothers when he was only nine. As an adult, Green's mix of gospel, pop, and soul has earned him fame and many hit songs, including "Tired of Being Alone" and "Let's Stay Together." Green is from Forrest City, Arkansas.

William Grant Still (1895–1978), a violinist and composer, grew up in Little Rock. In 1931 Still became the first African American composer to have his work performed by a major orchestra. For this and other musical firsts, Still is known as the Dean of Afro-American Composers.

◄ JOHNNY CASH

WILLIAM GRANT STILL ►

◄ HATTIE CARAWAY

POLITICAL LEADERS

Hattie Caraway (1878–1950) was the first woman to be elected to the U.S. Senate. She and her husband moved to Jonesboro, Arkansas, in 1902. When he died in 1931, she was appointed to finish his term in the U.S. Senate. Elected in her own right in 1932, Caraway represented Arkansas in the U.S. Senate until 1945.

Natural resources: fertile soil, forests, petroleum, coal, natural gas, bauxite, bromine, gemstones, granite, gypsum, limestone, marble, sand and gravel

Agricultural products: broilers, beef cattle, eggs, turkeys, milk, hogs, soybeans, rice, cotton, hay, wheat, corn, grain sorghum, catfish

Manufactured goods: animal feeds, canned vegetables, soft drinks, air conditioners, electric ranges, refrigerators, lightbulbs, televisions, cardboard, paper bags, tissues

ENDANGERED AND THREATENED SPECIES
Mammals—gray bat, Indiana bat, Ozark big-eared bat, Florida panther
Birds—bald eagle, Arctic peregrine falcon, interior least tern, red-cockaded woodpecker, Bachman's warbler
Fish—Ozark cavefish, leopard darter, pallid sturgeon
Reptiles—American alligator
Plants—pondberry, rose turtlehead, swamp thistle, snake-mouth orchid, royal catchfly, pineywoods dropseed, Arkansas meadow-rue, maple-leaf oak, French's shootingstar, hairy gramma, sedge

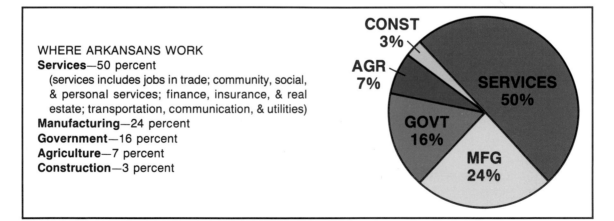

WHERE ARKANSANS WORK
Services—50 percent
   (services includes jobs in trade; community, social, & personal services; finance, insurance, & real estate; transportation, communication, & utilities)
Manufacturing—24 percent
Government—16 percent
Agriculture—7 percent
Construction—3 percent

CONST
3%

AGR
7%

SERVICES
50%

GOVT
16%

MFG
24%

Glossary

aquifer An underground layer of rock, sand, or gravel containing water that can be drawn out for use above ground.

civil rights movement A movement to gain equal rights, or freedoms, for all citizens—regardless of race, religion, or sex.

delta A triangular piece of land at the mouth of a river. A delta is formed from soil deposited by the river.

immigrant A person who moves into a foreign country and settles there.

lock An enclosed, water-filled chamber in a canal or river used to raise or lower boats beyond the site of a waterfall. Boats can enter the lock through gates at either end.

plantation A large estate, usually in a warm climate, on which crops are grown by workers who live on the estate. In the past, plantation owners usually used slave labor.

plateau A large, relatively flat area that stands above the surrounding land.

precipitation Rain, snow, and other forms of moisture that fall to earth.

Reconstruction The period from 1865 to 1877 during which the U.S. government brought the Southern states back into the Union after the Civil War. Before rejoining the Union, a Southern state had to pass a law allowing black men to vote. Places destroyed in the war were rebuilt and industries were developed.

reservation Public land set aside by the government to be used by Native Americans.

sediment Solid materials—such as soil, sand, and minerals—that are carried into a body of water by wind, ice, or running water.

treaty An agreement between two or more groups, usually having to do with peace or trade.

Index

Acknowledgments:

Maryland Cartographics, Inc., pp. 2, 11; Photo Source / Garry McMichael, pp. 2-3, 6, 13, 48, 51, 58, 71; Jack Lindstrom, p. 7; A. C. Haralson / Arkansas Dept. of Parks & Tourism, pp. 8, 12, 18, 53, 61, 69; Arkansas Dept. of Parks & Tourism, pp. 55 (top), 60; © Scott T. Smith, p. 9; Dixie Knight, pp. 10, 20, 41, 44; © Terry Donnelly / Dembinsky Photo, pp. 14-15; Stephen Kirkpatrick, pp. 16, 49 (inset); *Outdoor Oklahoma*, the official publication of the Oklahoma Dept. of Wildlife Conservation, p. 17 (left); Diane Cooper, pp. 17 (right), 42; Historical Pictures relating to the Louisiana Purchase issued by the *St. Louis Globe-Democrat*, 1902, pp. 21, 24-25; Library of Congress, p. 22; UCA Archives, pp. 30, 32, 37, 64 (top right), 65 (center right and left); Arkansas History Commission, p. 29; Fort Smith National Historic Park, p. 33; Arkansas State University Museum Archives, pp. 34-35, 35 (inset); *Arkansas Democrat-Gazette*, p. 39; Buddy Mays / Travel Stock, pp. 43, 46, 50; © Frank Siteman / NE Stock Photo, p. 45; Frederica Georgia, p. 47 (left); Root Resources: Garry D. McMichael, p. 47 (right), James Blank, pp. 56-57; © Connie Toops, pp. 49, 52; USDA, pp. 55 (bottom left and right), 57 (inset); Jerry Hennen, p. 59; Hollywood Book & Poster, pp. 62 (top right, left, center), 64 (top left); National Baseball Library, Cooperstown, NY, p. 62 (bottom); Milwaukee Bucks, p. 63 (top left); Baltimore Orioles, p. 63 (top right); Johnson Publishing Co., p. 63 (bottom left); Wal-Mart Stores, Inc., p. 63 (bottom right); Picture Collection, Special Collections Division, University of Arkansas Libraries, Fayetteville, pp. 64 (bottom), 65 (bottom); Maine South High School, p. 65 (top left); used by Abingdon Press with permission, p. 65 (top right); Jean Matheny, p. 66.